A Schoolgirl's Wa

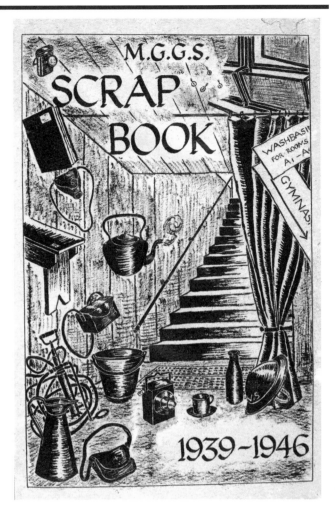

At the outbreak of World War Two, school art teacher Helen Keen started work on a remarkable collection of paintings and drawings. She set out to record, in paint and pencil, the lives of school children and their teachers as the war unfolded. Maidstone in Kent, where she worked, was effectively in the frontline with the Battle of Britain being fought in the skies overhead, and high explosive, incendiary and flying bombs all falling on the town and the surrounding area. For the children of Kent, the war years brought disrupted schooling, frequent air-raids, night bombings, and repeated visits to wartime shelters.

Miss Keen's paintings record it all. They are full of beautifully observed details, from the gas masks, lamps and stirrup pumps of wartime school life to the scribbled lines of vapour trails across the sky above. In particular, the artwork captures moments in time - a teacher bending to pick something up while rushing to take cover, a child holding on to her hat as she races downhill on her bike in an air-raid, an older girl lifting her book up to read in the dim light of the underground shelter. These evocative images together present a time in history from an unusual perspective, often with a defiant and wry humour, creating a powerful and unique tribute to the resilience of school children and their teachers in a time of war.

The paintings and drawings in this publication are all taken from Miss Keen's wartime scrapbook. They appear here alongside reminiscences of wartime pupils from Maidstone Grammar School for Girls, where Miss Keen taught, and from the King's Warren School Plumstead, which was evacuated to Maidstone. More than fifty past pupils, now in their 80s and 90s, have contributed to the research. Their accounts are often deeply moving and, where possible, have been left to speak for themselves. This book is their story.

"A place built for peace"

1938, the year before the outbreak of war, was a good year for Maidstone Grammar School for Girls (MGGS). The year began with a celebration of the school's Golden Jubilee. Even more excitingly, a magnificent new building was taking shape to replace the original Victorian building which had become seriously overcrowded.

Optimism about the future was strong. The school magazine recorded: *"The summer term of 1938 was full of suppressed excitement; there was an undercurrent of eager anticipation. Life would soon be so much easier, so much more pleasant. For were we not to exchange our cramped quarters for the grace and spaciousness of our new home?"* At last, at the end of the summer term in 1938, the new building was ready for occupation and a crocodile of pupils carried piles of books across town from the old school to the new.

At the opening ceremony, the headmistress, Miss Bartels, said she felt like *"Aaron leading the children into a land flowing with milk and honey."*

A sixth form student wrote: *"At last a dream has come true and we have a beautiful school to work in: a place built for peace, happiness and sunshine and all that we can desire."*

Left: The new school building

The school magazine continued in buoyant tone: *"We were free to taste the delights of our new surroundings, to feel the simple beauty of the building, to enjoy its peace and light … Our hopes had been realised. We had found inspiration and a stimulus to further endeavour, and it seemed that life would be fuller and richer."*

It is, of course, impossible to read these comments now without an awareness of their irony.

Below: Miss Keen's illustration of the front entrance of the new building

"Peace for our time"...

There was, in fact, widespread fear that another war was imminent. One pupil commented: *"We barely had time to settle into and appreciate our new surroundings when the Munich crisis cast a shadow over the country. I recall Miss Bartels touring the school one afternoon to inform each form that in the event of war breaking out, girls were not to attend school until further instructions were issued."* Ruth Hope (later Russell), another pupil, also remembered this time: *"I was literally petrified that there was going to be a war. Stomach-churningly petrified. I would not listen to the radio at home. I would go upstairs to avoid it. There was just this atmosphere. Everyone was afraid. When Chamberlain came back from Germany the first time, we were all gathered in the hall at school. It was all very solemn and serious. We were told if war broke out not to come to school. I remember going home and sobbing my socks off. I was literally terrified."*

It seemed, for a time, as though all would be well. At the end of September 1938, Neville Chamberlain returned from Germany declaring that "Peace for our time" had been secured. By August 1939, however, it was clear that the peace could not last. Gas masks were distributed, blackout blinds were fixed up in homes, and the evacuation from major cities was underway. Although it was a garrison town and therefore a potential target, and also rather obviously on an enemy flight path to London, Maidstone was considered a suitable destination for evacuees.

Mavis Hobday (later Goldsbrough), who had just left the sixth form at MGGS, remembered the evacuees arriving: *"All the 1938-9 sixth form pupils who had left school that summer were contacted and asked to report to the Agricultural Hall to help with the evacuees. I went with several of my friends and a number of staff were there too. We were put to work on the food stall, packing brown paper carrier bags with basic rations, one to be handed to each child as he/she left the hall with his/her foster parents. As to what we put in the bags I am a bit hazy... I think tins of corned beef, baked beans, pilchards, fruit and evaporated milk, and biscuits.*

The children I remember were ushered into the hall, gasmasks in cardboard boxes slung over their shoulders, name tags hanging round their necks, each clutching a bag (some just paper carrier bags) or a small suitcase containing clothes and precious belongings. Some had favourite soft toys. Even as an 18-year-old I was struck by how quiet they were. They must have been petrified.

They sat on the floor with walking space between the rows. The foster parents came and selected the child or children they fancied. At the end of the session there were a few miserable tired little wretches left. They were, I think, taken to a children's home. At the time I accepted what was happening as normal. It was only afterwards when talking with my mother, the horror of the situation struck me. It was almost as if the children were being put up for auction."

The photo shows Molly Kent (later Griggs), in the Guide uniform of the time. Many MGGS girls who were Guides were involved in welcoming evacuees arriving in Maidstone.

…"This country is at war with Germany"

It was at 11.15am on Sunday, 3rd September 1939 that Neville Chamberlain, the Prime Minister, broadcast the news that the country was at war: *"This morning the British Ambassador in Berlin handed the German Government a final note stating that, unless we heard from them by 11 o'clock that they were prepared at once to withdraw their troops from Poland, a state of war would exist between us. I have to tell you now that no such undertaking has been received, and that consequently this country is at war with Germany"*. MGGS pupils had differing, but equally vivid, memories of that day, each of which included a strong initial moment of panic.

Edna Abnett (later Dancy) was on holiday in Sheerness with her mother and sisters. They had chosen this Kent resort close to home because of the threat of war: *"We heard the speech on the radio in some small shop or restaurant on the sea front. My mother was perturbed and decided we should immediately pack up and go home. Just as we reached our lodgings, the air-raid sirens sounded - that dreadful wail. We had no idea what we should do; nor did the air-raid wardens who dashed up and down the street telling us to take cover! Eventually the All Clear signal sounded and we were able to pack up and get on a train to take us home. It seems that immediately after the declaration of war a small civilian plane was flying towards the coast from the Channel and the Coast Guard watchers assumed it was a German plane coming to bomb us."*

Other girls were still helping with evacuees. One was instructed that morning by her Guide Captain to help at a reception centre at a local school: *"Mr Chamberlain's speech was just beginning as I arrived at the school, and all stopped work to listen. After Mr Chamberlain's speech, the buzz of work started again, and suddenly we were quietened by a shout of 'Silence' from the warden. And then we heard it too - that horrible, sickening noise. The air-raid warning! We were bundled down some steps and into a coal-hole! We sat about, while all the time cold water dripped on us from above. That first half-hour of the war was a nightmare. As soon as the All Clear sounded and we had left our 'shelter', the first bus load of mothers and babies arrived. All the babies had good lungs, and they cried in unison until, one after another, they were packed off to their billets. Then came another bus load … and another bus load … Then there was one long rush of squealing babies and tired mothers until 7 o'clock. Our actual duty was to meet the bus and carry the babies for mothers while the Scouts took the luggage. I suppose we looked capable enough, or perhaps the mothers were tired, but they surrendered the babies without a word. I had never carried a baby before. At 8 o'clock I tottered home, very tired. But even then it was impossible to sleep in the heat kept in by the blackout curtains. That night, for a long time, I lay in bed, thinking of my first day of war, and still, when I shut my eyes, I saw babies."*

Another pupil was in church: *"At the end of the morning service at All Saints Church, Maidstone, we heard the air-raid siren. It was announced by the Rev Standen that we were at war with Germany. He said that we could either take shelter within the church or go immediately to some other safe place. We rushed to a nearby uncle's house and took refuge in their cellar."*

School attendance is disrupted

For the school, there was an immediate consequence to the declaration of war: the term could not begin as expected. With five hundred pupils and no air-raid shelters ready for them, the school was not allowed to have large numbers of children gathered together. Miss Bartels, the headmistress, took the only available course of action which was to postpone the start of term. She sent a letter to parents on 12th September 1939, two days before the term was due to begin. This is the opening paragraph:

"Dear Mr and Mrs _____
We shall not be able to open the school on Thursday, September 14th, as previously arranged. Will you therefore not send your daughter to school until you hear from us again and a definite date and time is given to you."

The receipt of the letter was a huge disappointment to Mary Robinson (later Smith) who was due to start that year and was really looking forward to it: *"I was devastated when we had a letter postponing the starting date to several weeks later."* Eventually, she was called in and told she was in Lower 3M: *"The M stood for 'morning' and for our first few months we went to school only occasionally and only in the mornings, when we were sent for. At that time very few people had telephones and so we used to be notified by a postcard. We never knew when it would be, and sometimes there were long intervals in between. Only basic subjects were taught - mainly Maths and English, no practical subjects at all. We were given lots of work to do at home and then we waited to be sent for again. The thirty of us lived in widely scattered country villages, so had no opportunity to get to know one another and make friends."*

New girls like Mary were divided into forms according to whether they lived in the town or the country. The staff made this arrangement with the girls' safety in mind: on the days they were called into school, all the country girls from the outlying villages attended in the mornings so they could return home safely before the complete darkness of the black-out. Town girls attended in the afternoons. Some younger pupils recalled coming into school for half a day only once every three weeks, lugging the contents of their school desk home again with piles of work to complete. Three weeks later they handed it in and collected more. In a postscript to her letter, Miss Bartels included some advice for parents: *"We urge strongly that you encourage your daughter to listen to the School Broadcasts appropriate to her age. These have now started."*

In the midst of all this disruption, teachers went out of their way to help as the school magazine recorded: *"During the Autumn Term, when the attendance of most forms was restricted to two or three half-days a week, some of the staff were kind enough to take small classes of well-behaved seniors in their own homes, and even, in some cases, went as far as to provide light refreshments."*

Throughout the war, the magazine maintained an upbeat tone, and this was true of its comment on part-time schooling: *"A great deal of time at school was lost, but the system was not without its advantages, as the amount of work which had to be done at home prompted self-reliance and gave greater scope to the individual. It is hoped that this year's results will be even better than those of pre-war years, even if General and Higher Schools candidates are disturbed during the examinations by the dismal sound of the air-raid sirens."*

Meanwhile, shelters were being urgently dug.

An evacuated school arrives...

Part-time schooling continued for many months, but MGGS pupils and staff were not the only ones affected as they waited for the shelters to be completed. The difficulties were also experienced by 240 pupils and their teachers from King's Warren School in Plumstead, who were evacuated to Maidstone to share the brand new school building at MGGS.

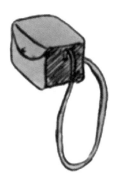

The upheaval in the lives of the King's Warren pupils and staff, and the resilience required from them, must have been significant. They had attended school in Plumstead every day since 28th August 1939, ready with their rucksacks or cases, gas masks and a day's food rations, waiting to be evacuated. Eventually, on Friday 1st September, after Germany's invasion of Poland, they were told they would be leaving by train the next day. One King's Warren girl, Sylvia Mapp (later Ling), remembered walking to Plumstead Station with her gas mask and a little case. She was 13 and said she felt quite excited because, at that stage, war meant little to her. They set off on Saturday 2nd September, having been told by one teacher to carry with them *"the infection of a good courage"*.

Edna Baker (later Sutton) remembered what they were each instructed to bring in their suitcase: pyjamas, a spare blouse, a spare pair of knickers, stockings, a liberty bodice with button-on suspenders, and a vest. The only other clothes she took were the ones she was wearing including her gymslip and hat. They were also told to take a two-pound bag of sugar for the family whose home they would share, and Horlicks tablets, nuts and raisins to eat on the journey. Edna didn't eat hers. She said *"I was brought up not to eat sweets or anything without being given permission and there was no one to ask in our compartment."*

When they set off, they had no idea where they were going, having been told only that it was somewhere in the country. All the station signs had been removed because of the threat of invasion. Their train was repeatedly shunted off the main track into sidings to allow for the movement of troop trains. Edna was 13 but had only ever travelled to Canvey Island before so a train journey was an exciting novelty.

Above: Edna Baker in her King's Warren gymslip and hat

On arrival, the girls were taken to MGGS and were delighted with the modern building, its huge playing fields and the views of the North Downs. But their journey was not yet over. They stopped for lunch at the school and then walked on to a local hall from where they were distributed to their billets - the homes of local families with whom they would stay.

Edna Baker remembered walking with a group of girls down one road, led by two adults. The adults had a list of names, house numbers and information about how many children each house was to take. As they walked down the road, they knocked at each door and deposited the right number of children. If they came to a house she didn't like the look of, Edna slipped to the back of the crocodile of girls. She said *"My two friends both had sisters so they were billeted together. Being an only child I had no one. I was very frightened and very lonely. Then a class mate I didn't know very well said 'Shall we go together?' I have never felt so relieved."* The anxiety they must have felt about their new homes is vividly apparent in the reaction of one girl who said that she could have cried with relief when her foster mother gave her a warm smile and invited her in. In a speech given later, the headmistress of King's Warren School thanked the families in Maidstone for the positive welcome the pupils received. She also praised the Mothers' Committee, four mothers who had come with them and who worked on solving billeting problems - either finding new billets if an arrangement was not working out, or settling difficulties in existing homes.

Many MGGS pupils had evacuees billeted with them. Families did not have a choice about this if they had room to spare. Some pupils were pleased with the new arrivals; others were not. One girl was distressed to be sharing a bed with three evacuees, whereas another girl, an only child, was delighted to have an evacuee "sister". Mary Robinson recalled her family's evacuees: *"In my home we had a girl of about 7 years named Beryl, but had not enough room for her 3 year old brother, so he was taken to live with another family further along the road. It is only since having children and grandchildren of my own*

that I've been able to really understand what a traumatic experience it must have been for them to be separated like that, so soon after being taken away from their parents. I never met Beryl's mother, but her father visited once or twice. Those children didn't stay very long - there were none of the expected air-raids for the first few months, so many parents thought that their families might as well be at home together. After that we had an older girl evacuee, Marjorie, and she came to school with me."

Photos above and below, courtesy of The Kent Messenger Group: evacuees arriving in Maidstone

Another girl remembered coming home to find three little boys about to enter the front door. *"They were evacuees from Plumstead, aged nine, eight and six. After they had had dinner, they went out to investigate the garden. I discovered them about to eat some deadly night-shade berries. Later they went out exploring and came back with their jerseys bulging with apples. That evening our evacuees were suffering from tummy pains."*

Sometimes evacuees and host families were astonished at how each other lived. Many London children were used to flush toilets and were shocked by the primitive conditions in some of the outlying villages. Houses there often had only a wooden toilet hut in the garden, with "night-soil" arrangements. Conversely, there were some evacuees who had never before taken a bath and were bemused that their foster families expected them to do so. Evacuation was a challenging experience for everyone.

For the King's Warren pupils, lessons began the week after they arrived in Maidstone, led by the teachers who had been evacuated with them. As the air-raid shelters were not ready at the school, their education was also disrupted and part-time. Classes for the junior girls were held just in the mornings in the local St Nicholas Hall. A school bulletin from the time describes a history lesson, a first-aid lesson, and a sewing lesson taking place simultaneously in different corners of the hall.

The girls are prepared for war…

Meanwhile, girls of both schools were being prepared for what wartime would bring. After the experiences of soldiers in the First World War, there was considerable fear that there would be gas attacks on civilians this time. Like everyone else, girls had to become accustomed to carrying a gas mask everywhere. The mask was kept in a square cardboard box with a long strap which was worn over one shoulder and across the chest. Gas mask drills at school became routine and some pupils found the experience very frightening. However, the masks had to be carried at all times, not just at school. They were fined one penny if they forgot them. Some tried to integrate their gas masks as a fashion accessory, making embroidered covers for them that matched their outfits when they went out.

Interestingly, pupils do not remember discussing why they needed gas masks - part, it seems, of a general desire to protect the girls by not talking openly about the war. In total across the country, 38 million gas masks were given out by September 1939. As it turned out, they were not needed.

Miss Keen often used her paintings and drawings to make an ironic comment on impractical wartime instructions issued to teachers. This was true of the illustration on the right. Kent Education Committee had issued a directive that pupils should be trained to work and play in their masks, and Miss Keen's sketches provide a humorous comment on what playing in a gas mask might have looked like.

On the left, MGGS pupil Dorothy Weedon and friends are pictured at play in a local orchard. The photo beautifully illustrates the instruction to take their gas masks with them at all times as two boxes can be seen hanging from a branch while a third hangs close to the trunk of the tree.

Photo, Courtesy of The Kent Messenger Group

The digging of shelters was the most urgent task at the beginning of the war. MGGS pupil Pat Hollis (later Wilmshurst) remembered the very first shelter which was at the front of the school: *"It was dug rapidly by a couple of old boys. We went down if there was an air-raid on the days we came into school. It had no lining to it. We used to look for worms coming through the walls. It just had an earth bench with a bit of wood along the top. It had one entrance and no exit. Near the entrance was a little partitioned area with a curtain, behind which were the spade and the pickaxe to dig us out if we got stuck down there. I didn't know that at the time. The staff were wonderful. They took us down there knowing that they might have to dig us out."* Many past pupils were full of praise for the calm composure of the staff which defused any sense of panic.

Some of the cloakrooms were reinforced early on to provide relatively safe refuges, and more underground shelters, also called tunnels or trenches, were dug at the front and the back of the school by gangs of men. One pupil was outraged at first: *"Imagine our horror when one day we came to school and found trenches all planned out with neat rows of pegs on our beautiful grass, of which we were so proud. Our next problem was the impossibility of being taught while the excavating machine was at work unless we had every window tightly shut."* Miss Keen's painting shows one of the entrances to the underground shelter at the back of the school.

In these concrete bunkers there were tunnels or corridors set at right-angles in a zigzag pattern. They were arranged like this to prevent a blast from travelling through the complex - or, as one pupil expressed it rather more frankly: *"The trenches were zigzagged so that if a bomb fell on one section it would only have wiped out that class."* The shelter at the back of the school had six zigzagged tunnels and three doors for entrance and exit, each down a set of concrete steps. There were also two escape hatches.

Each of these six tunnels had room for a class of thirty girls to sit on benches with their backs to the walls. When they were all seated, the knees of the girls on opposite sides of the tunnel would almost touch, particularly in the case of older pupils. Spaced at intervals along the zigzag were three tiny rooms. Two of these were probably used for storage, including for the shovels and pickaxes for use in an emergency. The third room was probably used for rudimentary toilets. The shelter at the back has been reopened recently, and there are some rusty curtain rails in the ceiling of this third small room, suggesting there were two curtained but very primitive toilet cubicles. One girl remembered the curtains were made of sacking. Electricity was supplied later, but in the first year of war the tunnels were lit only by lamps.

Evacuated pupils settle in at school…

In December 1939, four months after their arrival, the girls of King's Warren School celebrated their first Christmas away from home. As nothing had seemed to happen on the war front, the period sometimes referred to as 'the phoney war', some had returned home, but this was strongly discouraged. The majority stayed in their foster homes in Maidstone, and staff and older pupils made a great effort to give the younger girls an enjoyable time.

Like the MGGS teachers, the King's Warren staff were highly committed to the welfare of the girls and seemed to work throughout the Christmas holidays. Christmas parties, charades, films shows, carol-singing, games and competitions were arranged at MGGS for the evacuated pupils. At the junior party on Boxing Day there were traditional games such as Flipping the Kipper and Guessing the Picture, and country dancing. Supper was provided and there was a present for each child from the Christmas tree. At the end of the evening they joined in the Sir Roger de Coverley dance and sang "Auld Lang Syne". Prefects of both schools also worked together to organise a joint party for all the juniors on New Year's Day. Below are two verses of a song set to the tune "Run, Rabbit, Run", composed and sung by the King's Warren teachers at their Christmas entertainment. The last verse in particular gives a flavour of the positive thinking encouraged.

Come children, come children, come, come, come
Adolf a war has begun, 'gun, 'gun,
Leave your Plumstead homes and come away,
No longer here you can stay, stay, stay,
Plumstead and Eltham and Abbey Wood,
Give up your children so good, good, good,
They must now evacuated be,
Into the country so free, free, free.

Thus we have reached merry Christmastide
Pointing to gladness and peace worldwide,
Much we'd love to join our parents dear
In this season of all good cheer,
But from this place where we're put, put, put
We will not budge by a foot, foot, foot,
We are here to grow up safe and free,
And work for the new world that is to be.

Around February 1940, the shelters were finally completed. Part-time schooling continued a little longer for some, but by the start of the summer term full-time attendance had resumed for all. Even then, the two schools functioned separately, with pupils from each school taught by their own teachers.

There must have been an element of frustration for the MGGS staff and pupils that the presence of another school meant that once again there was over-crowding. The editor of the MGGS school magazine acknowledged the lack of space but, in the spirit of the time, made an effort to be welcoming: *"After one brief year spent in the luxurious spaciousness of the new school, we find ourselves again in cramped conditions. Every available inch is being used and even the laboratories and the gallery have become form rooms, for we are now sharing the building with evacuees from the King's Warren School. It would not be true to say that we hope their visit will be a long one, as the length of their stay depends on the length of the war, but we do hope that when they go back to London they will take with them happy memories of Maidstone and our school and meanwhile we gladly welcome them as our guests."*

The story of wartime evacuees has been well told elsewhere, but it is always stirring to hear about the children sent from their families to live with strangers. One King's Warren pupil, Kathleen Clarke (later Kay Preston), was 11 when she was billeted with a childless couple in Maidstone. They had taken in two evacuees, and Kathleen shared a single bed with the other girl. The couple were kind, but old-fashioned in their attitudes. Kathleen was sent to bed early and was not allowed the light on to read in bed. She came back to their house from school for lunch, when she had chores to complete. Letter-writing was often the girls' only link with home and she spent her 6d (six old pence) pocket money a week on stamps for letters to her mother and friends. Kathleen stayed away from her home in London for the school holidays, and through the course of the war was billeted with eight different families. She saw her mother only once and did not feel any of her foster parents had real affection for her. However, she made deep friendships. These were very important to her and a neighbour's child in Maidstone became a life-long friend.

Another King's Warren evacuee, Dorothy King (later Miller), said *" I wrote home regularly. The letters sound chirpy enough, but I know that sometimes I sat over them crying alone in the dining room. Used to a lot of attention from a protective mother, I was now, it felt, only a peripheral part of a strange family! I was often miserable."* Dorothy was much happier in a later billet, where she and another girl, Pat, lived with a Mr and Mrs Waller. Ivy and Bert, known as Aunty and Uncle to Dorothy, took their responsibilities seriously. *"We were splendidly cared for. Regular baths and hair-wash, regular and ample meals, clean clothes always to hand. It was as much our home as theirs."*

Above, Dorothy King on the left, with fellow evacuee and their foster parents, Mr and Mrs Waller

Left, the end of a letter sent by Dorothy to her mother in 1940, © Mrs D E Miller (Née King) IWM documents.6803

Mrs Waller wrote reassuring letters to Dorothy's mother: *"Dorothy is keeping well, and is not in the least bit worried over Jerry. It's a treat to see Pat and Dorothy reading or knitting in a raid… They are both very sensible and understand how things are, so don't worry over Dorothy."*

Edna Baker and another girl were first billeted with a family with a young baby. *"When I think back the lady was only about 23 years old. What a challenge and a burden for one so young."* Edna had three billets during her time in Maidstone. In the third, Edna was thrilled to discover there were two daughters close to her age. She had never had sisters before. They are still close friends more than 75 years later.

Looking back, Kathleen Clarke reflected on the stoicism of so many children: *"We were raised never to moan or complain and we were kept safe like that. We never cried. It was no great hardship in comparison to what others were going through, and there was no sentimentality. Hardship doesn't necessarily break you. It can be quite character-forming."*

Continuing preparations for the events of war

After the war had started and the dangers were better understood, further measures were taken to protect the safety of pupils. Sandbags appeared around the school and, to guard against injury from flying glass, splinter-proof netting was put up on all the windows. The netting was thick, coarse and cream-coloured and came in huge rolls. It was coated on the back with glue and stuck onto the glass. Some past pupils remembered rushing to the windows so they could pick at the netting during a lesson.

Miss Keen's vibrant illustration, dated September 1940, is full of movement and shows the process of protecting the windows being interrupted by an air-raid. The teachers hurry to the shelter, laden with the rolls of netting which they take with them so they can carry on cutting it up underground. The caption she gave to the picture reads: *"Windows ... Recurrent incident in the netting of"*. Miss Keen's paintings are often full of beautifully observed detail, and in this one the teacher in the spotted dress can be seen holding a pair of scissors at a very unfortunate angle as she runs down into the shelter.

Inside the building, brick blast walls were put up in the corridors at right-angles to the main walls, creating a zigzag route down the corridor. The aim was to prevent the blast from a bomb from travelling along the corridor, and was an idea developed from the experience of soldiers in the trenches during the First World War. Other walls, called "baffle walls" were constructed outside to shield windows. One pupil recalled men arriving early in 1941 with bricks, cement and sheets of asbestos to build the walls. Gradually the corridors were sectioned off giving more corners to turn and some of the windows became obscured. The school magazine referred to the new walls as *"formidable"*, and many felt a great sadness that this disfigurement was taking place in the beautiful "sunshine" building, opened so recently.

Life in the shelters

As soon as the shelters were finally ready, they were put to use. June Pickett (later Young) described the process: *"At the first wail of a siren all conversation in the classroom stopped. The teacher read out the number of the nearest staircase and the entrance to the air raid shelter from the notice on the door. Girls stood, picked up books and walked briskly in a silent single file as directed. The teacher left last, picking up the class register. The school was emptied in two to three minutes. The air-raid shelter was a zigzag concrete bunker under the playing fields. The teacher called the register and then resumed the lesson from exactly where it had been interrupted. When the All Clear sounded the process was reversed."*

Most girls seemed to have enjoyed going into the shelters, at least at first. Molly Kent recalled her experience at the age of 12: *"I well remember having lessons down there, although it was a much more relaxed atmosphere than the classroom! It must have been difficult for the teachers trying to instil knowledge into these very excitable girls. As soon as the siren went we had to evacuate the classroom as quickly as possible, and as soon as we reached the safety of the shelters out came the supplies that our mothers had given us to sustain us for a long time in the shelters. My mother used to give me Ovaltine tablets."* Other pupils remembered seeing a trip to the shelters as a welcome break. Most recall being more excited than frightened. As Margaret Amos put it: *"We used to think it was rather fun. Of course it was an absolute nightmare for the poor staff. I'm afraid we thought it was rather a joke. It wasn't a joke at all really, but when you're that age anything can be funny."*

When not having lessons, the girls were encouraged to sing to keep up their spirits, which they often did very loudly. Booklets with the words from popular songs were sold in Woolworths for sixpence, but the girls also made up their own simple songs, of which this is one example:

> *Down in the trenches*
> *On hard little benches*
> *We spend the live long day*
> *With stew on our knees*
> *And a nasty cold breeze*
> *The weather's cold and grey*

> *Chorus*
> *The siren goes – we all go down*
> *We're the safest in the town.*

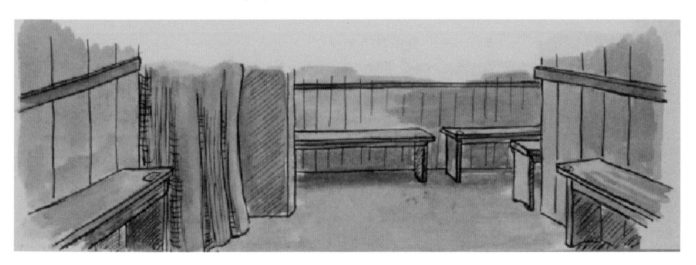

Miss Keen's painting above shows a corner in the zigzagged tunnels, lined with benches, where two corridor classrooms met. The concrete slabs that made up the walls can be seen, and the wooden rail was designed to keep the girls' backs from the wall in the event of a bomb falling in the vicinity. Girls were told they should not let their backs touch the concrete. The painting also shows the curtain which hid one of the little rooms where pickaxes and shovels were stored ready to be used in the event that the girls were trapped underground.

Uncomfortable …

The underground shelters were certainly not comfortable places to learn. The school magazine of 1940 admitted as much, though typically it presented the experience with a Dunkirk spirit: *"These labyrinthine vaults are not exactly cosy, and some people have been heard to complain of water dripping down their necks, but all the same, these expeditions to the underworld seem to be enjoyed by the majority, and now we feel prepared for any emergency."*

As Miss Keen's pencil drawing on the far left illustrates, the trenches were not waterproof. Pools of water would collect on the floor. Pupils variously remember the shelters as dimly lit, claustrophobic, eerie, airless, and with very hard benches. The girl pictured in the detail from a larger illustration appears to be having difficulty reading her text book in the poor quality light.

In winter the temperatures could be freezing. In cold weather, pupils carried their coats, scarves, gloves and hats with them all the time, ready for the eventuality that they would have to go to the shelters. In some ways, though, the pupils were better prepared for the cold than modern pupils would be as they had no experience of central heating, and there was usually only one fire, in the sitting room, at home. The winter of 1940 was certainly exceptionally cold. The illustration below was labelled by Miss Keen: *"Oh the long and dreary winter! Oh the cold and cruel winter!"* Girls can be seen carrying items for lunch through the snow, and heading towards the three separate entrances to the shelter at the back of the school.

In 2016, these past pupils returned to the school and sat in the seats they had first occupied more than 75 years earlier. It was a very emotional occasion.

Of course, there would have been at least thirty girls in each leg of the tunnel, so it would have been a lot more crowded, with little room for movement. This is demonstrated in the photo to the left which shows a modern class in the same part of the shelter. If a teacher wished to move down between the girls, she would call 'Legs Left' and the girls on each side would swing their knees to the left-hand side, opening up a gangway between them, as illustrated on the right.

One pupil remembered a particular occasion: *"One day the siren went while we were in the train coming to school, and so we did not hear it. When we reached school we were at once directed down the trenches. On that occasion the lights had fused and although there were torches at each corner, it was very dark in the middle, and so we had to grope our way along what seemed like miles of trench between girls, most of them with their legs stretched out, so that we were continually tripping. We finally came upon our form - who greeted us with cheers."* Her friends had been afraid that she had been caught in the raid.

An underground education…

Although there were times when pupils sang or played games, or just worked or read on their own, lessons certainly continued down in the trenches. It is hard to imagine the difficulties of learning in such circumstances. The trenches were positioned at right angles to each other with no doors between them, so classes in the neighbouring tunnels could be heard, particularly by the pupils seated at the corner who would be hearing two lessons at once. The school magazine of 1941 again found a positive on which to focus: *"Our powers of concentration should be strengthened by the difficulties of working with the efforts of the Lower Thirds at musical appreciation and other lessons going on at close quarters."* In most cases, the teacher stood at one end of the trench and addressed the pupils on the two long lines of benches in front of her. It must have been extremely hard for the teacher to make herself heard.

The concrete walls were often used as blackboards. This photo shows two modern-day pupils looking at an algebra lesson which was chalked on the wall of one of the trenches three-quarters of a century ago.

Other fascinating fragments of lessons also survive on the walls. One chalked sum appears to suggest that adding 66 and 26 makes 90. A past pupil pointed out, however, that it is a shillings and pence sum showing that 6/6 and 2/6 make nine shillings. Another chalked lesson is a puzzling shape belonging to neither Maths nor Science. A member of the modern PE staff eventually identified it as a drawing of a rounders pitch. It was probably chalked up when a games lesson was interrupted during an air-raid and then used to discuss tactics.

Some types of lessons were easier to teach than others. Several pupils remembered a lot of chanting of tables or French verbs. But surprisingly, there is evidence that science practicals were occasionally carried out and one girl certainly remembered an underground lesson dissecting worms. The addition of electric lights in October 1940 helped, making even drawing and sewing lessons possible. The girls were sometimes down in the shelters for several hours, not knowing when they would be released and, looking back, the past pupils were surprised how quickly they adapted to lessons in the trenches with books balanced on their knees.

Miss Keen illustrated the range of subjects that might be being studied simultaneously:

…while overhead The Battle of Britain is fought

While the girls may have treated the excursions to the trenches in a light-hearted fashion at first, the seriousness of the situation was brought home to everyone in Maidstone during the Battle of Britain when the sights and sounds of combat filled the skies overhead. Between 27th August and 31st October 1940, 234 high explosive and fragmentation bombs, ranging in size from 10kg to 250kg, fell on or near the town. In addition, there were thousands of 1kg incendiary bombs. The endurance of the pupils and staff at the school was severely tested and once again attendance was disrupted with girls coming in on alternate days.

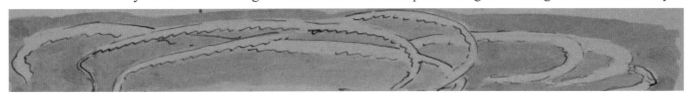

The heaviest raid on the town occurred just before midday on Friday 27th September when a squadron of German bombers flying at 10,000ft blasted the town. Damage stretched right across Maidstone, and there were 22 fatalities. Daphne Prett (later Baker), a pupil at MGGS, described that day in her diary: *"Slept until siren sounded and bombs were dropping at 4am. A two-hour loud raid. Bombs dropped on Chatham. Guns heard as I went to the station, but no warning. As school started the siren sounded and the raid lasted an hour. We came out of the shelters, but only until 11.15 when there was terrific gunfire. The siren sounded half an hour later! Bombs dropped on Maidstone. Springfield hit. The noise was deafening. We tried singing, covering our ears, chanting Latin verbs, but we couldn't escape. Our end of town escaped damage, but many lost their windows. We came up, starved, at 1.15pm. A late lunch then back to the shelter from three to four. Missed our normal train home. Another terrible night and lots of incendiaries were dropped."* There was also significant damage caused in the Marsham Street area of Maidstone a few days later on Wednesday 2nd October. Daphne's diary for the following day reads simply: *"Raids: 9 to 11am; 11.45am to 1pm; 1.15 to 2.30pm; 3 to 3.35pm; 4.35 to 5.15pm; 7.50 to 11pm; 1 to 6am Friday."*

In total, from August to October 1940, 53 Maidstone civilians were killed. No one from the school was hurt, but there had been direct hits on the railway lines on either side of the school site. This photo shows the devastation caused by a single bomber in Mill Street, Maidstone, on 31st October 1940. Several people were killed in the raid, business premises were wrecked, and the trolleybus system was severely damaged. Edna Baker was on a bus very close to the scene. She said: *"The bottom of the bus split and I could see the road underneath."* It is ironic that this particular day has gone down in history as the day the Battle of Britain was won.

Photo, Courtesy of The Kent Messenger Group

… and below, pupils carry on with their lives

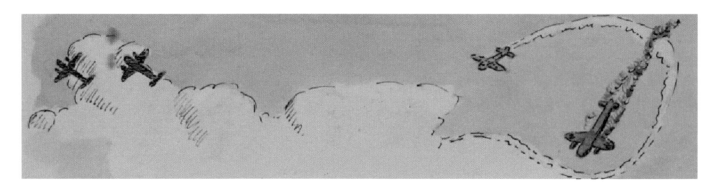

Even during the Battle of Britain, the girls continued to display an impressive resilience. Mary Robinson remembered more excitement than fear: *"The summer of 1940 was a dangerous, but exciting, time for us - the 'dog-fights' between British and German planes took place directly over the south-east. Vapour trails in the sky, the sound of aircraft engines and the frequent clatter of machine-guns led to a hail of spent cartridge-cases, and a rush of children to collect them as souvenirs. There were often as many as 10 warnings a day, with the occasional crash as a bomb fell or a plane was shot down, and the sight of white parachutes as pilots bailed out. Jagged bomb splinters (shrapnel) were also picked up, particularly by boys, who competed with each other to build the biggest and best collection."*

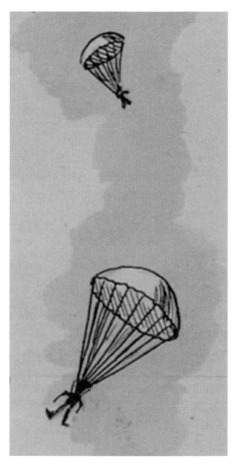

The girls became accustomed to going down into the shelters at school. Many felt very frightened if they heard planes flying directly overhead, but learned to hide their fear. In fact, several felt more afraid when they were at home as they perceived their parents' fear, whereas at school there was a feeling of camaraderie. Molly Kent said: *"I remember hundreds of planes coming over, looking up and counting them, hundreds of German planes, daytime raiding. At my age it was more exciting. We never thought we were going to lose although it was frightening at times. I had a little identification booklet with all the silhouettes of the planes, English and German. We got very, very clever at that. We could see what they were and would say 'Oh, those are Dorniers and those are Messerschmitts'."* Many girls also learnt to identify enemy planes from their sounds.

During a raid it was possible to hear shrapnel clinking down. Lots of children in the town would collect these fragments and there was a thriving trade in swapped pieces. At the time, Molly Kent had a boyfriend who fashioned a ring for her out of Perspex from the cockpit of a crashed aircraft, etching his name on one side and her initials on the other: *"I don't know if the Perspex was from a German or an English plane. It was like an engagement ring. He swore undying love to me. Next thing I knew, after the war, he'd emigrated to Australia."* Molly still has the ring.

The dangers for the pupils were very real. Several remembered machine-gun fire from planes as they crossed the bridge to school, or bombers overhead as they cycled along by the railway. Sometimes the planes were so close it was possible to see the pilots in the cockpits. One day, while pupils were in the shelters, a bomb fell on Maidstone barracks which was very close to the school. There was a tremendous noise and girls were shocked as the concrete slab in the roof of the trench which formed the door to the escape hatch rattled and jolted.

But they took the situation in their stride. Being in the shelters became a fact of school life.

Following official instructions

The official instructions issued to schools were often lightly mocked in Miss Keen's illustrations. The painting below pokes fun at the direction from Kent Education Committee that pupils should be trained to follow their teachers.

HAD WE CARRIED OUT OFFICIAL INSTRUCTIONS....

1. "The pupils should be trained to follow their teachers." K.E.C.

The teachers in the painting appear to be carrying out this instruction by bribing the pupils with food, in the same way as one might train a dog. The teacher in the foreground is carrying a large plate loaded with cake and fruit, and bars labelled "Chocolate" can be seen protruding from her gas mask case:

The teacher leading the column of girls behind her is flourishing a bag labelled "Buns":

The humorous nature of the picture suggests that Miss Keen did not think the girls needed to be trained like dogs. In fact at MGGS the pupils reported that the teacher was always the last to leave the classroom en route to the shelters, not the first.

The painting also appears to show the girls running, and some falling as a consequence. The girls were actually told to walk not run, unless, according to one pupil, *"there were Messerschmitts overhead. Then we were allowed to run. I can remember doing a mad dash several times."*

Dinner in the shelters…

School food during the war was generally considered to be good, and, with families coping with rationing, the school meal was usually the main meal of the day for the pupils. A particular favourite was the day when the main course was a big jug of thick soup. This appears to be the meal being served out in Miss Keen's vivid painting below.

DINNER IN THE TRENCHES, 1940.

Steamed puddings were a frequent feature of the meals, including one topped with jam that was referred to as 'dead baby.' Semolina was common too and towards the end of the war a fortified orange jelly was served. Pupils were told they should not complain about their dinners and were expected to eat everything that was served to them.

Problems arose when a raid started during lunch time. One pupil remembered: *"It meant carrying a plate with food on it whilst walking briskly. This was difficult with peas, which rolled off."* Another pupil recalled a pale green jelly *"which we christened slaked lime and cabbage water. I ate it because I was hungry. One alert, we went to the shelter, rushing for cover with our slithery jelly. My friend's jelly wobbled onto the floor and sat there quivering and covered in loose cement dust. Nonplussed, she scooped it up in her fingers, scraped off the dust and proceeded to eat it."*

A sixth former, writing in the school magazine, described occasions when the siren went as they were eating. At first they left their dinner to get cold, but learned pretty quickly to seize their plates as they hurried down to the trenches. When they had finished they would sit, playing games or knitting, waiting for "Moaning Minnie" - the All Clear signal. This sixth former acknowledged the efforts of Miss Booth, who ran the kitchen, and the other kitchen staff in preparing meals in such conditions.

If pupils were already in the shelters as dinner time approached, the kitchen staff brought the meal down to the trenches. Pat Hollis remembered the process of serving out: *"The cook - she was tiny - used to stagger in with a huge iron pot full of hot stew or casserole. Then the other maid used to bring in the plates and we had to get off the benches so they could line them up on the bench and dollop out the plates of food. They were absolutely wonderful people to go to and fro, bombers or no bombers. We were jolly hungry and it was beautiful food."*

Pat remembered only ever being in the shelters at the front of the school, so the cooks had to carry the food all through the school building to those at the front, as well as serving those in the trenches at the back. The kitchen staff did not take cover until a red alert which meant that aircraft were in the immediate vicinity.

Winnie Bowles, who is pictured in the photo on the right, worked in the canteen from 1937 to 1964. Her own account of meals delivered to the shelters provides further evidence of the dedication of the canteen staff: *"Our first real 'ups' and 'downs' started when the war broke out. It was then we started 'going down' and 'coming up' from the trenches, and as business had to go on as usual, it was nothing to see the canteen staff trekking off to the trenches with a bowl of carrots, or onions, or apples, or rhubarb, that had to be prepared for the next meal, and Miss Booth and Margaret had to keep popping up to the kitchen to see that the roast beef was not cinders, or the potatoes were not mash, or that the rice puddings were not burning.*

Life was never dull in the trenches, and sometimes we learned a little French or German, and sometimes we were just interested in a singing lesson when the All Clear sounded and back to earth we had to come, and I'm afraid our lessons were soon forgotten when we arrived back in the kitchen and 15 or 20 minutes had to be made good. I can remember one afternoon we had quite a long session in the trenches and when we arrived back in the kitchen there were some 'mopping up operations' to do, as I had left a tap running and the water was finding its way under the kitchen table. It took us nearly half an hour to mop it up."

Some pupils were hungry at home and their mothers struggled to feed them, particularly to provide sufficient protein. Dorothy King, a King's Warren evacuee, learnt to eat a broader diet. *"I had been a rather faddy child but (partly because I was too scared to do otherwise) I ate everything and found I was enjoying things like tripe and onions, 'chitterlings', mashed swedes – all of which I would once have been very reluctant to try."*

The stews and puddings at school were an important source of nutrients and calories. The school magazine recognised this: *"In an insecure world, when all else might be in doubt, dinner appeared with unfailing regularity; the faithfulness of the canteen staff never once failed us."*

Dinner time ditty

This rhyming verse appeared in the school magazine for 1948, but looks back to dinner time in the shelters during the Battle of Britain. It paints a dramatic picture in words of dinner being served underground during an air-raid, and also strongly conveys the importance of the midday meal.

The siren went at half-past eight
Just as we entered through the gate;
We've done some French, our sums were wrong,
We felt they would be all along;
The map of Norway, chalked on wall
Does not excite us, not at all,
For we are in the trenches,
Sitting on hard benches
And we think it's dinner-time.

Let's sing a song; let's sing "John Brown";
Let's shout it till the roof comes down;
Let's find some cards and play at "Snap";
Let's close our eyes and take a nap;
Let's go visit round the bend,
And see who's at the other end
Of these eternal trenches,
For we're tired of these hard benches,
And we know it's dinner-time.

But hark! The noise aloft is done,
The prefects and the staff now run;
They run to fetch the plates and mugs,
The knives and forks and water-jugs,
They run to fetch the starving, food,
They run to bring us something good
To eat down in the trenches,
While we sit on hard benches
All agog for dinner time.

The staff and prefects re-appear;
We greet them with a rousing cheer,
For they have brought us steaming stew,
Cabbage and boiled potatoes too!
Be quick and pass the helpings, please,
That we can balance on our knees
Down in these chilly trenches,
Sitting on hard benches,
For we're sure it's dinner time.

Now let us eat; now let us feast,
For we were starved, to say the least -
What's that? More banging overhead!
Our hearts sink down; they sink like lead,
For well we know, amidst that thudding
No staff can fetch us any pudding
To eat down in the trenches,
These wretched, gloomy trenches,
Tho' it's now past dinner-time.

Let's pass the plates, let's pass the forks,
Let's pass the dreary hour with talks
Of better times before the war
When we had dainties served galore;
Ice-cream, bananas and fruit-pie
With sugar piled on, inches high
Before the days of trenches
And sitting on hard benches
Every blessed dinner time.

Another lull! And up they spring.
Oh, bring us biscuits, anything -
We'll not complain; we'll eat it all,
Both portions big and portions small,
And then we'll tidy up the place
And bring out books from every case
For lessons in the trenches,
Sitting on hard benches,
For we've had our dinner time.

But first let's do what we've been taught,
Now let us pause while in thought,
And let us spare a tiny space
To offer up a little grace;
Planes may be fighting overhead,
But we are safe, we are fed.
Let's give thanks then in these trenches,
As we sit on hard benches -
That we still have dinner-time.

Home life for MGGS pupils was significantly affected too. Many girls were moved around because of the war, sometimes with significant consequences for family life. Ann Salmon (later Hill) was sent initially from Maidstone to stay with her grandparents in Surrey, but returned four years later to start at MGGS in 1943. She said *"I was very happy with my grandparents and I did not want to come back to Maidstone. In those four years I had grown apart from my parents. I didn't know a soul at school when I came back. I'm sure my mother felt it too. Those four years, life in the village and with my grandparents, were the happiest years of my childhood. I only saw my parents once every six weeks."*

Home was not quite the secure place it had once been for anyone, and most houses had some sort of shelter. Beryl Honney (later Mackenzie) had a Morrison shelter, which was a large indoor metal cage with wire mesh sides: *"It was a double bed size with a springy base just off the ground. We had it downstairs in the lounge, and my father painted it a glossy cream colour so that it was quite presentable. During the worst of the bombing I slept in there and my mother would join me if there was a raid. For daytime sheltering we used the pantry, which was under the stairs - considered the safest place in the house. We put our food in a cupboard outside and squeezed chairs into the pantry. My mother and our lodger would sit in there during raids knitting balaclava helmets for the troops."*

Other families had an Anderson shelter at the bottom of the garden. This was a shelter partly submerged in the ground. The top section was above ground and covered with soil. Some families shared a shelter with their neighbours, and the digging of it had often been a joint venture. Sometimes there were bunkbeds in the shelters for children and chairs for the adults. Anderson shelters proved to be very uncomfortable in winter and subject to flooding. Other families used a reinforced larder or a cupboard under the stairs. Many girls slept in a shelter or cellar or under the stairs throughout the Battle of Britain.

Several girls experienced direct damage to their homes. Mary Robinson, pictured left in her school uniform, recalled an incident one night: *"Two parachute mines fell on our village putting the gas works out of action and demolishing a large detached house near us. Many houses were badly damaged. It happened during a raid which had not seemed particularly threatening - no sound of gun-fire, but these mines fell silently, so we had no warning. Some plaster from the ceiling fell on my head and mother said urgently 'get in the cupboard under the stairs'. I did and plaster from the walls fell on me in there. We soon went into the shelter together with next-door neighbours. Daylight revealed the extent of the damage - dozens of houses with windows shattered, doors blown off and roof tiles smashed or displaced... The whole village was without gas for some time."*

There was also a continuing fear of what might happen to family members serving at the front. Girls would sometimes watch the telegram boy to see which house he had a message for. There were few phones, so a telegram was the method used to inform families of a death.

The war experienced beyond the school …

Of course, the war affected all pupils in their lives outside school. With the Battle of Britain being fought in the skies over their homes across the summer and early autumn of 1940, every girl had first-hand experience of wartime events. The following accounts appeared in the school magazine of 1941 and again give evidence of a remarkable capacity to adapt to extraordinary events. The first is from a girl aged 15:

"I do not think I shall ever forget one Thursday morning in the Autumn of 1940. It was a bright morning, but intensely cold, and it was one of our 'off-days' from school. The siren had sounded, and no one had taken much notice. I was just about to switch on the wireless, when I heard the most awful noise - a low rushing sound ending in a screeching whistle. I ducked instinctively, and the rest of the family made one dive for the cellar. We expected to hear a terrific explosion, realising by now that it must have been a bomb. We heard nothing, however, but a dull thud. Plucking up courage, I opened the door and walked down to the gate. You may imagine my surprise when I saw, not two hundred yards from me, sticking out of the ground, the tail fins of a bomb! With a couple of leaps I was back inside the house and telling the news to the rest of the family.

By this time there was a tremendous hue and cry going on outside. Police and soldiers were hurriedly erecting barriers to stop the traffic. A neighbour informed us that there was another bomb in our back garden. My grandfather promptly toddled off up the path to find out just exactly where it was, whereupon my grandmother was in a great 'state', declaring that he would be blown up at any moment. More alarming reports were circulating by now, and we discovered that we had at least thirteen time-bombs around us. Although we now feel a certain pride in having a bomb in our back garden, it scared us all badly when it happened."

This second account was written by a 12 year-old:

"I was rudely awakened from my sleep by a vigorous shake from my smaller sister, 'Incendiaries! Incendiaries!' she shouted, jumping like a cat on hot bricks. 'Where?' I exclaimed, leaping out of bed, now fully awake. I dashed to the window and drew aside the blackout, and I was astounded at the scene which met my eyes. 'Hooray, it's fairyland; hooray, it's fairyland!' chanted my sister. Indeed, if I had not known that there was no such place, I should have believed her. Tiny glows of light lit up the dark outlines of the trees, like so many fairy lanterns. Over six hundred incendiaries were dropped. Later I collected some of the wings of the bombs, painted them, and sold them for our Barnardo fund."

Travelling to and from school could also have its dangerous moments. Pupils were told that if a raid occurred while they were walking home, they should take cover under a hedge, or knock on the door of the nearest house and ask to be taken in. If they were on the train going home from school they should draw the blinds as protection against flying glass, and lie on the floor of the carriage under the seats.

All the girls were witnesses to the destruction caused by war. Many saw evidence of the bombing of London's docklands. Barbara Osborne (later Hughes) recalled: *"My dad used to go up to Covent Garden to take soft fruit for the big hotels and the first night he went, the Germans bombed the docklands and he got stuck in it and I think that frightened everybody in my family. We could see the flames in London from my bedroom window. You could see a whole red brilliant area. It was frightening - when it was your father who may not come home."* Mary Robinson also watched as the docklands burned: *"The flames could be seen for miles, warehouses full of spirits, sugar, wood and other inflammable goods blazed fiercely. We lived a good 30 miles away, but I can remember standing outside the house to see the red glow in the sky to the north-west."*

Ruth Hope said: *"I remember being very upset about what I heard about London, the bombing, the fires, the incendiaries, but we used to hang out of our back bedroom window and watch the dogfights overhead and cheer when one of the Nazi planes got shot down. I remember hanging out of the window one beautiful day, vapour trails all across the sky, watching these dog-fights going on. My mother had been in Maidstone when bombs were dropped on Mill Street. She came hurrying home. 'Come down,' she said to us, 'Come down. Don't you know it's dangerous? They're dropping bombs on Maidstone.'"*

Hop-picking in the fields gave several pupils a good view of the Battle of Britain. There was a shortage of the traditional labour for the hops. Londoners came down as usual, but without their menfolk, many of whom had been called up or were fulfilling essential roles in London either in their jobs or as volunteer firefighters or air-raid wardens. Even those who came ended up worrying about what was happening to their homes in London, and many did not stay long. Local women and children stepped in to fill the gap. Molly Kent remembered: *"I did go hop-picking in 1940 in the Battle of Britain. It was fascinating watching all the fights going on overhead. At one time, one of the German planes was shot down and we all cheered. The German pilot parachuted out and came down in a hop field and of course his parachute got caught in all the bines at the top. The men all went off with pitchforks."*

June Pickett also remembered hop-field scenes and the exuberance of children observing the battles in the sky: *"There was no direct danger to the people on the ground except from bits of falling metal. The fighters were too busy with each other to look at anyone below them. During these 'dogfights' the boys stood on the hop-bins and cheered on our side as if they were watching a football match. Adults were more discriminating, and when planes disintegrated in the air, or fell helplessly to the ground, would ask, 'theirs or ours?'"*

Many pupils witnessed damage to the streets around them. The photo on the right shows a house in Paradise Row, Maidstone, destroyed by enemy action in September 1940.

There were also other changes around the town which emphasised the danger for everyone. Because of the fear of invasion, huge ditches were dug on the outskirts of the town and concrete blocks appeared in various places, designed to stop tank movement and the landing of troop-carrying gliders. Military personnel manned the roads in and out of town.

Photo, Courtesy of The Kent Messenger Group.

A teacher's perspective…

Doris Ayres taught English at the school. She was a widow, her husband having been killed in the Spanish Civil War. She was the only teacher with the title 'Mrs' as, remarkably, there was still a marriage bar on women in education until 1944. Mrs Ayres left a record of her wartime experience at the school, and had vivid memories of school life in the shelters: *"As I generally arrived at school about 8.00am it became my duty to take the lamps down to their hooks (in the shelters) each morning. I usually descended the steps with some trepidation; there might be a German paratrooper. Raids became so frequent that the girls grew indifferent to danger. They would saunter down the drive in the morning, disregarding our frantic signals to run for shelter.*

We spent as long as seven hours a day in the trenches, the staff flitting 'overland' from one section to another at change of lessons. Often delayed by an Alert, we would arrive to find our next class conducting its own lesson, using the trench walls as blackboards. Dinner-hour leisure in the trenches was enlivened by impromptu pantomimes, variety shows and card games. When bombs were heard falling we shouted 'Heads forward', and obediently the long rows of children bent forward on their benches, away from the walls in case the vibration should split and batter their heads. When we had time to think about it, we were amazed at the cool courage shown by our pupils."

She remembered a particular conversation with one pupil…
"Helen, your homework is not given in; kindly explain."
"Sorry, Mrs A - but my book is under the ceiling."
"What do you mean? Of course it's under the ceiling if you've left it at home."
"I mean - a bomb has brought down the ceiling and my book is underneath."

…and also one specific episode that happened on 31st October 1940:
"One day, a stray plane dropped a stick of bombs through the centre of the town. Miss Cooper arrived at school late. She had been walking along Mill Street when the bombs fell. A warden had yelled to her to lie down close to a wall, but - 'I just knelt; you see I had my best coat on.' In the wrecked street several people were killed - a miraculous escape for our Mathematics teacher."

In looking back from the present, past pupils recognised it must have been a very trying time for the teachers. They admired their teachers for ensuring that everything seemed so organised and there was no sense of panic. As one past pupil expressed it: *"Nothing ever ruffled the staff. They were absolutely fabulous, utterly composed."*

This little picture of Miss Keen's appears to show staff in the trenches relaxing during the dinner-hour. A lot of knitting seems to be going on.

Miss Keen produced this beautifully observed painting of teachers resting back-to-back in the trenches in September 1940. The caption beneath it reads: *"There passed a weary time."*

A rhyming verse, included in Miss Keen's scrapbook, gives a light-hearted take on a teacher's experience of life in the shelters. At one point in the verse, the All Clear provides a welcome release from the difficulties of teaching underground:

"But, joy, oh rapture! - don't you hear
That lovely noise, - the blest All Clear?
It fills the air. - Push back the benches,
Hooray! Again we leave the trenches.
The sky, the sun, the birds, the trees -
Who can tire of looking at these?
But best of all it is to see
The staffroom's joy, - a pot of tea

We fill our cups with steaming cheer,
We sip a sip, - and then we hear
A hooting, tooting, mooing moan,
A sound the most alarming,
It is indeed that ghastly thing,
The cursèd Bull of Barming*!
With sighs and groans we turn and run
Snatching first, a lamp, a bun…."

*The Bull of Barming refers to the air-raid siren nearest to the school

…and back they go to the shelters again. Teaching in Maidstone during the war required a great deal of patient endurance.

The milk problem…

Every morning at break-time, the girls lined up to receive milk and buns. The buns, Devon Split, Chelsea, or Belgian, were 1d (one old penny) each, and were very popular. The milk cost 2½d (two and a half old pence) a week. Each child received a small bottle of milk containing one third of a pint. Given food rationing, it was considered particularly important that school pupils received this milk during the war.

In November 1941, The Board of Education delivered a circular to schools entitled "The Milk in Schools Scheme" containing the following notice: *"The Board have already indicated … that increasing difficulty must be expected in obtaining supplies of school milk in one-third pint bottles. The capacity of our bottling plants is affected by shortage of labour, the use of unskilled labour and by difficulty in their operation during black-out hours. The bottling of milk in one-third pint bottles also absorbs a disproportionate amount of labour, materials and transport. For these reasons … a large proportion of the school supplies must be delivered in pint or quart bottles or possibly larger containers."*

The circular also gave advice to schools about how they could measure out a third of a pint for each child, and said that *"the amount of time which teachers with commendable zeal are already giving to the distribution of school milk must therefore … be increased."*

In response to this, Miss Keen produced the sardonic painting opposite, mocking the advice which she transcribed underneath, and showing how long the queues of girls would become while they waited for teachers to measure out their milk if they used the method advised.

Later, Kent Education Committee distributed powdered milk for schools. The humorous painting below demonstrates exactly what Miss Keen thought of that.

DRIED MILK.   The K.E.C. decides, and will take no denial.

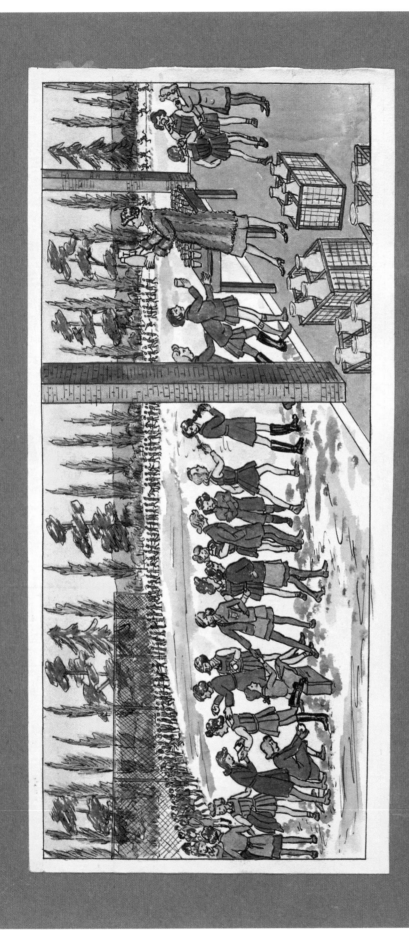

...illustrated

HAD WE CARRIED OUT OFFICIAL INSTRUCTIONS.....

3. "Instead of using a one-third pint measure, milk in pint or quart bottles can be measured into cups with sufficient accuracy by holding a stiff paper scale against the bottle with the same effect as in pouring from a graduated medicine bottle."

Extract from B. of E. Circular, November, 1941.

More of the same at school

The Battle of Britain officially came to an end on 31st October 1940, but this did not bring an end to the need for the shelters at school. Attacks became less frequent and less intense, but the sirens sounded in Maidstone almost every day between 1st November 1940 and 27th June 1941.

Meanwhile, girls at the school continued to cope with other wartime problems. One difficulty was the severe shortage of paper. Barbara Hughes remembered: *"We had to use our rough notebook right to the end, take it to the teacher and she would say 'Yes, you've filled that up. Now go and rub it out and start again'."* The school magazine reported *"A new rough notebook is rapidly becoming a thing to wonder at"* and Pat Hollis commented that *"getting a new rough book felt like pinching the crown jewels."* Pupils also had to make sure they wrote in all the margins. Sometimes, when they had finished an exercise book, teachers would make pupils turn the book upside down and write between the lines, filling the book again from back to front. The paper they did have was poor quality and had flecks of grey in it. Old rags had apparently contributed to its manufacture. There were other shortages too, for example of tennis balls, batteries, paints for art, and material for needlework.

Pupils were encouraged to contribute to the war effort in a variety of ways. They tended class allotments on the school site, and the vegetables they grew were used in the kitchens. Some girls were sent to collect stinging nettles from the banks of the railway, although this was discontinued when the nutritious stinging nettle soup turned out to be unpalatable. Some girls spent their games lessons hoeing local sugar-beet fields, and, in the holidays, children were encouraged to *"Dig for Victory"*, or to *"Lend a hand on the land"* gathering apples, cherries, beans or blackcurrants. A local farmer had permission to use the precious school field for some of his sheep.

Various items were collected: rose-hips to be made into a syrup for babies; paper and card for re-pulping; bones for making glue; food scraps for pigs and chickens. Thread was collected to use in embroidery kits distributed to wounded soldiers and prisoners of war. Pupils who were Girl Guides learned how to make a fireplace out of rubble or how to make a cup of tea using an old paint tin. Some knitted, unpicking old jumpers to make new ones. Others wrote letters to soldiers. Yet others minded children in a nursery while their mothers were engaged in war-work.

The shortage of labour for hop-picking meant that at times stacks of hop-bines were brought into school for the girls to strip. This photo shows pupils in their science overalls engaged in this task at the front of the school. It seems that beer was considered an essential commodity in wartime.

There had been doubts raised from the start of the war about the wisdom of choosing Maidstone as a destination for evacuees. Some London County Council members had understandably disapproved of the decision. The King's Warren girls, evacuated to MGGS, had certainly experienced air-raids in the same way as the MGGS girls. In 1940, their second year at the school, a traditional carol concert was arranged for them on the Friday before Christmas. The fourth year pupils were in the middle of singing "In the Bleak Midwinter" when the air-raid sirens sounded and everyone decamped to the trenches. The service continued underground, with carols sung unaccompanied, and ending with "The Holly and the Ivy". It was a carol service which few would forget.

In January 1941, London County Council members came on a tour of the area. As reported in *The Kentish Independent,* they found the children generally happy and well provided for. One girl was quoted as saying *"We should like to see our mothers oftener, but, except for that, everything is very good."* But some London County Council members concluded that coastal counties were unsuitable for evacuees. As the newspaper reported: *"They were inclined to ask whether areas in which shelters were necessary were the best in which to billet evacuees between 5 and 16."* The acting chairman of the Council was blunt in his comment: *"The children are in districts on the direct route of German planes."* The photo below shows King's Warren girls enjoying a picnic on the Downs near Maidstone in the summer of 1941.

Eventually, on 8th September, after two years spent at MGGS, the King's Warren girls were once again at a station with cases, haversacks, coats and gas masks as they started a fresh evacuation journey, this time to Bedford. For many it was a very sad occasion, including for those Maidstone foster parents who had grown to love their foster children. Edna Baker was devastated. *"As well as being separated from my parents, I also had to move from my adopted family."* The editor of the MGGS school magazine shared the sadness but celebrated the effect of their departure: *"We were sorry to lose the King's Warren School as a spirit of friendly co-operation had grown up between the two schools. It is, however, a joy to be able to revel in the vastness of our new buildings as we did in the year before the war."*

It is interesting that many girls who started as King's Warren pupils in 1939 never had lessons in the school's Plumstead building throughout their school days. They were educated entirely in Maidstone and Bedford. Their evacuation from Plumstead was fortunate, however, as their school building was severely damaged during a bombing raid in September 1940. Edna Baker remembered Miss Summers, the headmistress, being nearly in tears as she told them of the bombing during an assembly at Maidstone.

The photo shows King's Warren pupils examining their damaged school on their return in 1945.

At various times during the war, some pupils from Maidstone were also evacuated, including some to America and Canada. Fourteen MGGS girls went to Whitchurch near Cardiff in 1944, but all had returned within a fortnight. The vast majority of girls stayed in Maidstone throughout the war.

Fire-watching duties

One very surprising aspect of wartime school life is that older girls were entrusted with the highly responsible role of fire-watching at school in the evenings and at weekends. The task of the firewatchers was to look out for incendiary bombs and, if they burst into flames, to extinguish the resulting fire before it could take hold.

The bombs were small and hundreds were dropped at a time. They would catch fire on impact. The girls were relieved at night and then would cycle home. This is the list of instructions given to the pupils who took on this role:

Duties of Firewatchers

1. Know where all stirrup pumps and water are to be found and how to use them.

2. How to summon help if required (office telephone and internal telephone)

3. Do the blackout of the entrance hall, B1, B2, kitchen and dining room. See that doors of staffroom and staff cloakroom are shut.

4. On Wednesdays and Sundays (when night-watchman does not come until 9pm) go <u>all round</u> the school, opening the door of every room to see that no lights have been left on, and see that each of the outer doors, except front door, is locked.

5. If unable to do a promised duty, or find a reliable substitute, inform the mistress in charge. If you wish to leave before 9pm you should still tell the mistress who is coming on for the night, so that she may come earlier. Do not go until you have been relieved.

Fire-watching duties also included going out onto the roof, from where there were spectacular views over Maidstone, and of the night sky. Across the town there was a very strict blackout, with cloth, paint or thick paper being used to cover windows.

There was one rich benefit from the darkness that many pupils appreciated: the whole sky above Maidstone was full of stars, a sight you would not be able to see so clearly now. Many girls had star charts and learned the names of the constellations they could see.

The school was led throughout the war by Ruth Bartels. She is something of an enigma. She was a passionate supporter of education for girls and yet was an intimidating figure for most of her own pupils. One said *"I can sum her up in one word - terrifying."* Misdemeanours which could attract a serious telling off included being seen without a beret in town. She did not let standards slip despite the war and would accept no excuse for failing to have biscuit-coloured socks. If these were not available, then white ones had to be dyed in tea. June Pickett remembered her sister being asked by Miss Bartels why there was a black ink line down an English essay: *"She explained that a bomb had gone off and she had jumped. 'Don't let it happen again,' was snapped back. My sister was furious and suggested to Mother that the Head should have a word with Hitler instead of blaming her."* Dorothy Weedon remembered Mrs Bartels sending her to run a mile home to fetch a forgotten lunch ticket. As she ran the mile back again, an air-raid began and shrapnel rained down on her, but she was much more frightened of being late for Miss Bartels than of being hit by shrapnel. On that occasion it seems that Miss Bartels may have regretted her own strictness as, when Dorothy arrived back at school, she found the headmistress waiting anxiously in the drive to hurry her down to the safety of the shelter.

However, despite the harsh exterior, some pupils detected other qualities. Edna Abnett remembered an event which took place while she was in the underground shelters: *"In my Latin class we were translating a passage from Virgil in the Aeniad, the part dealing with the Trojan Wars and we had just come to the description of the Greeks emerging from the belly of the Trojan Horse when a line of bombs was dropped through the town, whumph, whumph, whumph…..! It was just before lunch, and when the All Clear siren sounded those of us who went home for lunch prepared to depart. The headmistress sent for me and said she would drive me home, knowing that at the time I was staying at my grandmother's. She also knew (presumably she had been in touch with the police or defence people) that one bomb had fallen dangerously close to the army barracks across the road from Granny."*

Mrs Ayres also saw this compassionate side of the headteacher: *"Miss Bartels would never allow a pupil to go home alone if it was thought that the home might have been damaged during a raid. She would make a personal visit, leaving her car to pick her way on foot through broken glass and rubble to satisfy herself that the particular house was intact."*

Doreen Crump (later Slot) had a different reason to be grateful to Miss Bartels. She had lived in Deal and had watched the soldiers returning from Dunkirk. Her family had been involved with the rescue of troops. She said she had been traumatised by this event and felt an overwhelming sense of insecurity, desperately fearing an immediate invasion. The family moved to Maidstone and Doreen was interviewed by Miss Bartels for a place at the grammar school. She had had little schooling, but Miss Bartels took her in despite her lack of mathematical knowledge. Doreen said that the school was a lifeline for her and helped her to heal: *"The amount of care for us was wonderful."*

It is certainly true that Miss Bartels faced unprecedented challenges in running the school during those years. June Pickett concluded: *"It was recognised that the Headmistress and her staff made abnormal conditions seem almost normal, and reduced Hitler to an irritating nuisance."* The school magazine of 1948 paid tribute to Miss Bartels: *"Fortunate in having at our head one whose courage and determination never wavered in the face of difficulties - and few know just how many and how great they have been - we gratefully acknowledge leadership so inspiring."*

Then the doodlebugs come...

Eventually, there was a stronger sense of optimism about the progress of the war. D-day took place on 6th June 1944. Past pupils remembered the build up to the Allied invasion of enemy-occupied France, repeatedly asking their parents *"Will it be this weekend?"* Once the invasion had started, older pupils followed the progress of the troops by wireless and through the press, some cutting out and saving maps that were printed in the papers. They could only see moving images of the troops at the cinema.

But then, suddenly, there was a new and terrifying threat. June Pickett remembered being woken one night by *"a loud, harsh engine like a clapped-out motor engine."* All that could be seen was *"a fiery tail, like a comet, moving across the sky. The next day the ugly shape making this ugly sound could be seen. It was a pilotless bomb with wings and an engine, and was quickly dubbed, 'The doodlebug'."* These flying bombs, or doodlebugs, had a distinctive engine sound and when that stopped, the bombs crashed to the ground within a few seconds, causing significant damage and often loss of life.

Many girls never forgot their first doodlebug sighting. One pupil remembered her father saying *"'There's a fire rolling across the sky.' I was frightened out of my mind. All night I imagined a ball of fire."* Molly Kent said *"I remember the first one coming over. We were all standing outside looking at it. We thought 'what the hell is it?' So I went to school but they told us we had to go home. I think we went the next day and they told us they were flying bombs. But I think we called them doodlebugs because if you give something a funny name, then you're not so scared of it. A flying bomb sounds awful, but a doodlebug sounds better."*

The first doodlebugs fell on 13th June 1944. Margaret Fullagar (later Thompson) recorded doodlebug activity in her diary during the following weeks:
"Monday 19th, Tuesday 20th no school again because of Aerial Activity.
21st had usual lessons but mostly in (room) A8 in case of air raids.
23rd did not go to school because of doodlebugs.
26th had English exam a.m. Geog. p.m. Had to go to trenches 3 times because of doodlebugs. Quite nice paper.
27th had Geometry exam a.m. Went into trenches 3 times. Biology exam p.m. Not too bad. 28th no school a.m. Because of doodlebugs.
July 1st (Saturday) watched doodlebug shot down. Super.
July 10th not much going on except doodlebug exploding in air.
The entry for 10th July in particular shows that even doodlebug activity became accepted as normal. Many past pupils remembered the thrill of watching Spitfire pilots nudging the flying bombs with their wings to tip them off course.

The doodlebugs proved to be perhaps the most severe test of the resilience of those at school, and of their ability to adapt. June Pickett described the way the school dealt with the threat, a process illustrated on the opposite page by Miss Keen:
"It was impossible to use the school air-raid shelter against this almost continuous activity so an alternative had to be found. The teachers took turns to sit on a chair just outside the front door. At the first sound of a doodlebug she ran in and rang the bell. Teachers and pupils grabbed their books and went down on the floor with heads under the desks. As in the concrete bunker the lesson proceeded without a pause. When the doodlebug had passed there was no need for a second 'get up' ring. After a number of these yo-yo movements a girl said,
'Please Miss Griggs, what is the use of my head being under the desk if the rest of me is cut off?'
'Don't be silly,' was the answer, and, 'Have you all got your maps?'

June then gave an amusing picture of what it must have looked like as each girl sent up an arm in a brown jumper to find the map left on the desk: *"To anyone passing the classroom it would have been weird to see thirty brown-clad snorkels waving around to locate a map."*

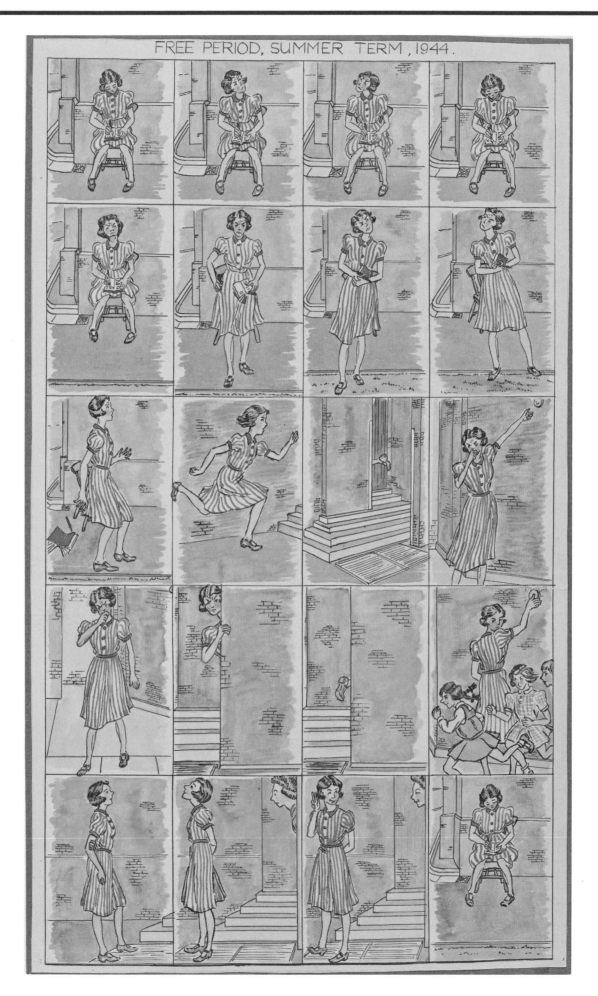

FREE PERIOD, SUMMER TERM, 1944.

The impact of doodlebugs

Many pupils had direct and frightening experience of the devastation doodlebugs could cause. Mary Robinson remembered a particular occasion in her village: *"On August 5th (1944), just before 7pm, there was a tremendous crash close by and I set off on my bike to investigate. The sound had come from the opposite end of the main village street and as I went towards it I met people looking shocked and dishevelled - one woman carrying a baby in a blood-stained blanket. The road was strewn with broken glass and debris and a cloud of dust, and a smell I shall never forget, hung over everything. A doodlebug had fallen demolishing a number of houses and badly damaging many more. Of course there were people killed. I was soon sent away, and people trained in rescue work and first aid arrived to do what was needed."*

Mary was also taking public examinations at the time. *"I was in my final year, taking School Certificate exams, and we were told to attend school only on the days when we had exams. If the air-raid siren sounded during an exam we had to go to the shelter and stay there to complete it - anything but ideal conditions."*

A PLACE

OF

SAFETY.

MIDSUMMER, 1944.

Pat Hollis's experience was slightly different. She is the pupil in this picture. Pat said she was in fact doing an exam paper under the desk not reading a book: *"A doodlebug went over. The sirens went off and I took my Latin subsid paper underneath the desk. Miss Hewitt was invigilating and waving to Miss Keen sketching in the corridor. I don't know how the poor examiner managed to read my writing."*

Although it is hard to imagine doing oneself justice in such conditions, Sheila Preece (later Ormerod) found an advantage in sitting an exam during the doodlebug raids: *"There was no time to go to the shelter: we had to get under our desks. I was doing Oxford Entrance when a doodlebug came over and I had just finished one question so the time under the desk gave me a bit longer to plan the next one."*

Individual experiences

While the pupils shared similar experiences in school, many also had their own distinctive stories to tell.

These are two such stories:

One Saturday in 1944, a doodlebug exploded near the church in the village where June Pickett lived. The next day, June helped to clear up the damage: *"While clearing an area near the main door, I saw a stranger come into the church. From top to toe his clothes were new and matching, unknown in England at that time. He looked like a stage character from the twenties. His flat peaked cap, half-belted jacket and plus fours were in a gingery brown with an overlaid check. His thick stockings ended in highly polished brown laced shoes. Most startling of all was the split second gleam in his eyes as he saw the damage.*

His statements and questions, in a very slightly accented voice, were contradictory. He said he was hiking from the next village and had seen the doodlebug explode. It had fallen the previous day; his spotless shoes had never seen dust or mud; and his small, black, rectangular rucksack had never carried squashy sandwiches or bottles of water. Years later I read an article about Hitler wanting to know how the doodlebug was performing. Being short of man power he was employing amateur volunteers as spies.

The man's questions were specific. Did the bomb just fall? Had it been shot down by a gun or plane? Did it explode before or on impact with the ground? Did it fall in a straight line or in a spiral? And so on. He sensed my unease and left. I found the Vicar clearing the altar and told him of my concern, but he was busy and did not bother about it. I went back to the church and stood thinking. I could phone the police and leave them to find out whether he were innocent or not. If he were a spy he would be shot, and I would be responsible for his death. I decided I would not be able to live with that possibility and so did nothing, but I have spent the rest of my life feeling like a traitor."

Of course, there was also tragedy. In 1941, Edna Abnett was preparing for her School Certificate: *"My world fell apart, however, shortly before these exams. My father was killed on May 20th. I shall never forget the feeling of devastation and helplessness. At the age of not quite fifteen, one assumes these things only happen to other people, a silly assumption given what was going on around me. I was quite unable to talk about his death, and I found sitting through the exams that came so soon afterwards an agonising experience.*

He was killed during the defence of Crete. The ship was machine-gunned from the air and he and five others died. My Uncle Cecil visited us unexpectedly the day the telegram came, staying until it arrived. My mother was convinced that he knew what had happened and wanted to be with her, but he never admitted it. He worked at the Admiralty, receiving signals from the ships, so he almost certainly knew something. My father's ship had been in several battles already, the most notable being the first battle at Narvik. We already knew that he had been awarded the Distinguished Service Medal for bravery in that action.

Fortunately, the young are very resilient, and gradually my life came together again. But profound changes occurred in the family. In addition to the personal loss, my mother had to find work in order to make ends meet, and as she had not worked during her married life, she started at the bottom. There had never been much money and now there was less. And there was no longer a man who came home from time to time and fixed things that needed fixing. My father's mother suffered enormously; not only had she lost her son, she had lost her only child. My sisters also suffered. For me, his death overwhelmed me again in September when my mother and I went to Buckingham Palace to receive his medal from the King."

Fire-watching...

As the war appeared to be nearing its conclusion in 1945, the practice of nightly fire-watching was brought to an end. Miss Keen's richly detailed illustrations accompany a two-page tribute to MGGS's "Fire-watcher in chief". The name of this individual is not known. The end of the verse implies she was given a lamp as a fitting gift: the illustration at the foot of the second page shows that the fire-watcher can now replace her functional lamp and record book, for a soft lamp and books to read for pleasure.

A LAMP FOR A LADY.

When you are old, and nineteen forty seems
Gone like the fag-end of disturbing dreams,
Perchance you may forget how once you kept
A constant vigil here

while Maidstone slept,

And, with your rota of devoted wenches,

Made good the boast

that "Britain never blenches".

Let us remind you then of shell-lit skies,

And siren songs

that oped our sleepy eyes;

The illustrations show a stirrup pump in the top left-hand corner of the first page. This was a portable device used to extinguish small fires. In the top right-hand corner of the second page, the fire-watcher is in action with the pump.   It was so-called as there was a stirrup at the base of the pump on which the fire-watcher has placed her foot to steady the device while she pumps. The verse, composed by someone unknown, does not match the illustrations in quality but is revealing of this particular wartime role.

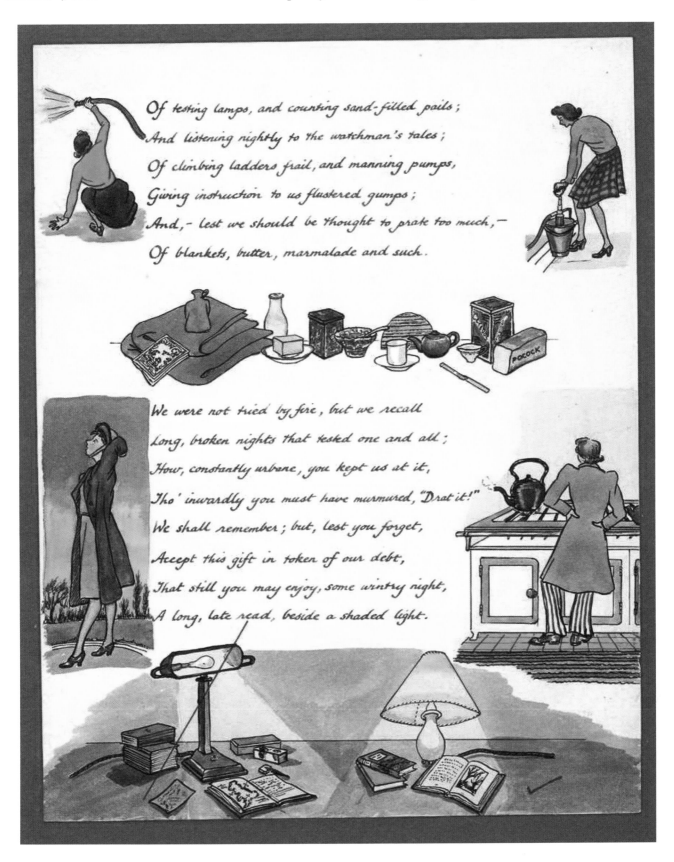

Of testing lamps, and counting sand-filled pails;

And listening nightly to the watchman's tales;

Of climbing ladders frail, and manning pumps,

Giving instruction to us flustered gumps;

And, - lest we should be thought to prate too much, -

Of blankets, butter, marmalade and such.

We were not tried by fire, but we recall

Long, broken nights that tested one and all;

How, constantly urbane, you kept us at it,

Tho' inwardly you must have murmured, "Drat it!"

We shall remember; but, lest you forget,

Accept this gift in token of our debt,

That still you may enjoy, some wintry night,

A long, late read, beside a shaded light.

A miscellany of attitudes to the enemy

Many pupils commented that the war was never discussed in school. They had no memories of references to the soldiers or prayers for them. Some felt it was an appropriate policy to protect them from the horrors going on in the world, whereas some others felt they were protected too much. Contemporary attitudes to the enemy amongst the pupils are interesting. The following are all comments made by past pupils of MGGS in 2016, looking back at the prevailing attitudes of themselves and their parents:

"We learnt French for the first year, and then added German – we wondered if we were going to be invaded and we were being prepared."

"I remember being given the option of learning German or Latin. I chose German because I thought it would come in handy if we didn't win the war."

"On one occasion, we were sent to pick fruit for the war effort and we were tactlessly practising our German much to the annoyance of the women whose sons were in the Forces: 'Speaking that language while our sons are being killed by the Germans! You ought to be ashamed of yourselves'."

"When there were enemy aircraft overhead and we were sheltering under a desk, we used to giggle about learning German while they were trying to kill us."

"There was fear of an invasion. Daddy said he'd shoot me if German soldiers got me."

"My mother said that if the Germans invaded she would take me and my sisters down to the river and drown us."

"I can remember Hiroshima. It was my father's birthday. We thought it a wonderful present. Looking back, I see it so differently. It's difficult to remember how much we hated the Germans and the Japanese. It lasted a while. The father of a friend would never buy a Japanese TV."

"My father was horrified to think both his daughters were learning German. Having been in the army in WW1 and there we were in the middle of WW2 fighting the same enemy, I suppose his feelings were understandable."

"We were brain-washed that the Germans were fiends, that they would bomb non-military targets. When I saw the damage to Munich after the war, the devastation to cathedrals and other buildings, I was shocked."

"Everybody was controlled by newspapers which spoke of wicked Huns and wicked Germans. There was no Beethoven, no Mozart, no Goethe."

VE Day at last…

Finally, in the summer of 1945, the MGGS school magazine celebrated the end of the war, exultantly calling itself the "Victory Magazine", and adding *"Surely it is a triumph that, in spite of the paper shortage, we still have a magazine in which to record VE Day!"*. Victory in Europe Day took place on Tuesday, 8th May, and the magazine reflected on what that meant for the school:

"The announcement of Victory in Europe came in time to give us two complete days' holidays. During those two days we gave ourselves up to the joyous celebrations of thanksgiving services, floodlights, bonfires and fireworks, but once back at school, our thoughts have turned to the last five years, as they have affected our school-life, and looking back, we must marvel at our own good fortune. Unlike so many schools, we are still one community, unbroken by evacuation; in spite of air-raids the school itself still stands, the same beautiful building that thrilled us when it first opened in 1938. Certainly there were temporary hardships, in the shape of lessons in the trenches and overcrowding… The war has affected us enough, for us to be determined that it shall never happen again if we can do anything to prevent it."

June Pickett vividly described her memory of the celebrations: *"When it was announced on the radio that the war in Europe had ended, there was a burst of spontaneous jubilation in towns and villages. In front of my house the road became full of men. Someone produced a football and a game with no sides, no goal posts and no rules surged up and down the road. The local policeman took off his hat and jacket and sat on a step happily blowing his whistle for no apparent reason. I wondered whether I would ever again feel so alive when for so long being alive could not be taken for granted."*

Miss Keen's painting above captures the scene as the netting is removed from the staffroom windows. The caption reads *"VE Day -1, 8.30pm approx"*.

...a time to celebrate

Pupils shared their experiences of VE Day and their joy in the 1945 school magazine. A sixth former spent the day in the capital:

"At a quarter past six I awoke with a sense of great expectation on this the Greatest Day in Europe for nearly six years - VE Day. It was fine and bright, and the very air was charged with excitement.

On reaching London I began to enjoy the expectant bustle everywhere. A frequent sight was that of people who, celebrating in advance, had lost their last trains, slept in the parks or revelled till dawn, and were only then making their way home, a little crumpled, but exuberant. We headed for Piccadilly Circus, walking through Kensington Gardens and along Oxford Street, and joining one of the several crowds gathered around loudspeakers in Bayswater Road to listen to Mr Churchill's speech. Our progress was somewhat slow, for everywhere were singing, dancing, cheering people in mufti and every conceivable type of uniform - 'brass-hats' lifting grubby children above the heads of the mobs; exultant American servicemen offering chewing-gum to ladies who, although dressed in the height of fashion, looked a little bedraggled.

Day turned to evening, and as dusk closed down on a wildly happy London, bonfires began to blaze, and the sky was aglow with their light. Those who had them, let off fireworks, some brandished flaming torches, and a youth flung ticker-tapes and newspaper 'confetti' from the back of a Trafalgar Square lion.

Then came what was to me the most enjoyable moment - that of seeing the great buildings and the happy faces of the city illuminated by floodlights. Drab offices became white fairy palaces; the majestic buildings of Westminster were bathed in soft light; flower-beds and trees in the parks were ablaze with colour, and everywhere was glory. With this picture of London in my mind, stamped unforgettable to the end of my days, I close my diary on a memorable day in history."

A fifth-form pupil wrote about more local celebrations:

"The morning passed in hanging out flags, preparing a picnic tea, and feeling very elated. Punctually at three the family collected solemnly in the drawing room and heard the Prime Minister. After that my friend and I started out on our cycle ride to Brenchley. It was very hot, and most people were indoors, in fact we saw very few people indeed; the largest gatherings seemed to be outside churches. The only sign of jubilation was the flags which festooned the houses. We ate our tea in a field yellow with buttercups, at the bottom of Brenchley Hill. As we lay looking up into the oak leaves above our heads, we heard the bells of Brenchley Church chiming, so we stirred ourselves and toiled up the hill, and down to the Church. Leaving our bicycles outside, we entered the porch.

It was like walking from an oven into a cool cellar. Right inside it was even cooler, and a quiet air of thankfulness and peace descended over the crowded congregation. The service was short, but very sincere, and ended with the hymn 'Abide with me.'

When we returned, we listened to the King's speech, and the salutes which preceded it. Outside, the dusk settled, and I went out to feel the coolness of the evening. There was not a sound. Before 9 o'clock there had been dancing in front of the village inn, but now silence covered the valley and seemed to rise from the river with the white mist. There was a glow of bonfires in the west and a few searchlights played across the sky."

Reflecting on the end of the war many years later, Edna Abnett wrote: *"The dead did not return to life. Some of the wounded did not recover. Some of the missing never returned. Some disrupted lives never got put together again. The bombed houses did not miraculously get replaced or repaired. But with the end of the war, there was hope; we had been through a very hard time and things could only get better."*

It was an unusual consequence of war that cleaning windows became a cause for celebration. Miss Keen painted pupils enthusiastically at work on this task, and balancing in a variety of ways to do so, on *"VE Day +2"*. The school magazine reported *"And now at last the safety net has disappeared from the windows, torn down by fingers which had been itching to do it for years. We see parties of girls in overalls walking round the school with bowls of water and window-cleaning materials. Willing volunteers have been clearing away sand-bags and other means of defence, which we no longer need."*

The dried milk is disposed of

Miss Keen continued her strand of ironic drawings immediately after the war by showing the barrels of milk powder that had piled up in the school. The drawing has the caption *"Milk Powder Plot 1946"*.

MILK POWDER PLOT, 1946.

She then painted the scene as staff tried to crush the solidified lumps of dried milk powder:

-AND THE OUTCOME OF IT!

The end of the blast walls

The victory magazine of 1945 celebrated the end of the netting on the windows and the removal of the sandbags around the school, but added sorrowfully: *"Soon only the blast-walls will be left, and I am afraid that these are beyond our powers to remove."* The blast - and baffle - walls were considered a final disfigurement of the beautiful school building, which was still only seven years old as the war ended.

It was not until 1948 that the magazine reported: *"It is significant, and indeed typical, of the sympathy and co-operation of the parents that it was by their initiative and labour that the blast walls, the last accompaniments of war to remain within the school, were demolished."*

Miss Keen's illustrations of this process echo this praise of the efforts of parents, but also suggest some dissatisfaction with the contracted labour brought in to remove the walls:

The picture of the fathers and daughters opens to reveal their effective chain of effort:

"Peace, perfect peace"

In 1948, the school magazine looked back on the war years which had seen *"the construction of trenches, the blocking up of some windows and netting of others, the building of the blast walls. The trenches became more and more familiar. We had lessons in the trenches, milk in the trenches, dinner in the trenches. As the war years passed, we were exposed to what was perhaps the most disturbing and exacting of our experiences, the menace of the flying bomb. But that too passed. In retrospect we can rise above the discomforts of those days and reflect upon the degree to which we did succeed in maintaining a certain continuity in our corporate life. That the fabric of the school remains almost intact is a matter for deep thankfulness. And it is encouraging to discover that much persisted which we held, and still hold, to be of value."*

The set of photos on this page, taken in 1946, marked the return of ordinary school life, unconstrained by sirens, air-raids and overcrowding. The bottom right-hand photo shows an Art class in progress. In the centre of the picture in the light-coloured overall, Miss Keen, whose artwork has illustrated this book, can be seen helping a pupil.

The war had come to an end, and life could return to normal. As one girl put it: *"No more carrying overcoats wherever we went, to put on down in the trenches, and no more interrupted lessons or meals. Peace, perfect peace."* But the past pupils who have contributed to this book have never forgotten their wartime schooling.

The painting below shows the blocking up of some of the shelters in 1948. Fortunately, the shelter at the back of the school was not blocked up and was re-discovered and re-opened in 2013.

It is with this picture that Miss Keen's exquisite scrapbook of paintings and drawings of school life in wartime comes to an end.

The End of the Trenches, 1948.

This has been a story in which there has been fear, uncertainty, disruption, and danger. It is hard for those of us who have not lived through such times to imagine the difficulties faced in running a school during those six long and extraordinary years, particularly through the Battle of Britain and the doodlebug attacks. It has certainly put my own experience of school leadership into perspective. It is also hard to conceive what it must have been like to teach or to attend school as a pupil knowing that terror may fall from the sky at any moment. I have deliberately kept my comments to a minimum in the telling of this tale, as Miss Keen's contemporary illustrations and the accounts from the past pupils are strong enough to tell their own stories. In this final paragraph, however, I would like to pay tribute to the immense resilience, spirit and courage of these wartime schoolgirls and their teachers. I am in awe of their powers of endurance and their seemingly unfailing good humour. Their accounts are profoundly moving and inspiring, and it has been an honour to bring together in this book those stories and Miss Keen's beautiful illustrations.

Mary Smith

Acknowledgements

I would like to offer my deep gratitude to the "old girls" of Maidstone Grammar School for Girls and King's Warren School who have so generously shared their memories with me. I have been privileged to visit and interview many in their homes. Others have shared reminiscences by phone, email and letter, including messages from America and Australia. Some are quoted in the book, but the contributions of all have been invaluable in helping me to build up a picture of school life during wartime.

In this list of wartime pupils who have all helped me, original surnames are in brackets.

MGGS:

Elisabeth Alexander (Tye)
Sheila Amies (Beaufoy)
Sue Barnes (Perkins)
Jean Bentley (Kemsley)
Margaret Amos
Valerie Boyd (Gould)
Janet Coe (Waters)
Jeanne Corbin (Farmer)
Daphne Crabb (Robinson)
Ann de Garis (Emby)
Edna Dancy (Abnett)
Marion Dulson (Shales)
Valerie Edrich (Brenda Ponder)
Sheila Enfield (Ruler)
Joyce Everson (Bailey)
Eunice Foley (Milner)
Shirley Foss (Carter)
Joan Godfrey-Jull (Relf)

Mavis Goldsbrough (Hobday)
Valerie Gooding
Jill Gradwell (Watts)
Molly Griggs (Kent)
Margaret Hinks (Cooper)
Barbara Hughes (Osborne)
Theresa Knight (Garnet)
Eileen Knowler (Osborne)
Una McKeand (Hobday)
Beryl Mackenzie (Honney)
Inga Mayor (Armstrong)
Adriane Norris (Blunden)
Sheila Ormerod (Preece)
Carol Pringle (Lovelidge)
Ruth Russell (Hope)
Ann Salmon (Hill)
Jeanne Smith (Sloman)
Doreen Slot (Crump)
Mary Smith (Robinson)

Jennifer Snell (Strike)
Beryl Sutton (Ashby)
Berenice Tallett (Burchill)
Margaret Thompson (Fullagar)
Brenda Tilley (May)
Jane Turner (Thomas)
Barbara Wadmore (Banks)
Brenda Wallace (Gosling)
Dorothy Weedon
Betty Wicken (Hart)
Audrey Wilkinson (Minns)
Pat Wilmshurst (Hollis)
June Young (Picket)

KWS:

Sylvia Ling (Mapp)
Dorothy Miller (King)
Kay Preston (Kathleen Clarke)
Edna Sutton (Baker)
Frederica Winter

Thanks are also due to Daphne Baker (Prett), Mary Edwards (Watts), Doris Ayres and Winnie Bowles who left records elsewhere; to all the unnamed contributors to MGGS magazines during and after the war; to the King's Warren Old Girls' Association; to the Snodland Historical Society; to the Imperial War Museum; to Lila Brewer; to current MGGS headteacher Deborah Stanley for the original idea and for her consistent support of the project; and to Michelle Starns, PA to the headteacher, for her unfailing and invaluable assistance in the creation of this book.

In particular, we are all indebted to Miss Helen Keen who created such a detailed and evocative record of wartime school life in her "scrapbook". She was a quietly-spoken, unassuming, but inspiring teacher of Art. Her art room was immaculate; when pupils came in for lessons there were always beautiful objects in the display case. She had an enamel plate on her desk which held moss into which she pushed all manner of small bits and pieces she had gathered - tiny wild flowers, sprigs of fern, twigs with small leaves or berries, pieces of evergreens, small stones. Miss Keen is remembered for her distinctive Eton crop hairstyle and her equally distinctive calligraphic handwriting. She was also responsible for the large bowl of flowers and foliage that used to grace the polished table in the centre of the school entrance hall.

Her scrapbook of paintings and drawings is a rich gift for us all.

Mary Smith